VAMPIRE CASTLE

Anne Rooney

CLASH

Copyright © ticktock Entertainment Ltd 2008

First published in Great Britain in 2008 by ticktock Media Ltd,
2 Orchard Business Centre, North Farm Road, Tunbridge Wells, Kent, TN2 3XF

ticktock project editor: Sophie Furse
ticktock project designer: Sara Greasley
ticktock picture researcher: Lizzie Knowles

With thanks to series editors Honor Head and Jean Coppendale

Thank you to Lorraine Petersen and the members of nasen

ISBN 978 1 84696 705 4 pbk

Printed in China

A CIP catalogue record for this book is available from the British Library.

Picture credits (t=top; b=bottom; c=centre; l=left; r=right):
[apply Pictures]/ Alamy: 27b. Jack Carey/ Alamy: 20c. Jim Clare/ Nature PL: 28. dpa-Film Zephir/ dpa/ Corbis: 8.
Everett Collection/ Rex Features: 23. Lisette Le Bon/ SuperStock: 13, 21. Mary Evans Picture Library/ Alamy: 25. D.
Parer & E. Parer-Cook/ Ardea: 29t. Photos 12/ Alamy: 16, 17b, 22c. F. Scott Schafer/ Corbis: 10. Shutterstock: OFC,
1, 2, 6-7, 7t, 10-11 background, 11, 12, 14-15, 16-17 background, 18br, 19t, 20-21 background, 20b, 22-23
background, 26-27 background, 27t, 28-29 background, 30-31 background, 31t. Daniel Smith/ zefa/ Corbis: 18l. Volker
Steger/ Science Photo Library: 26. ticktock Media Archive: 4-5, 29b. Visual Arts Library (London)/ Alamy: 24.

Every effort has been made to trace copyright holders, and we apologise in advance for any omissions. We would be pleased to
insert the appropriate acknowledgments in any subsequent edition of this publication.

CONTENTS

VAMPIRES

Stories of vampires have been told around the world for hundreds of years...

...but do vampires really exist?

VAMPIRE CASTLE

It's late. It's dark.
You are lost in the mountains.
The wind howls.

Should you shelter in the castle?

You knock on the door and it opens.
No one is there, but a meal is ready.

It seems you are expected!

Suddenly your host
appears from nowhere.

He shakes your hand.

His hand is as cold as ice.

He watches while you eat.
But he eats nothing.

You try not to stare at
his long teeth, and
pale skin...

...but he looks so
very, very strange!

Your host leads you to a bedroom.

You are so tired that you lock the door and fall asleep right away.

In the middle of the night a noise wakes you. There is someone in your room – it's your host!

**The door was locked.
How did he get in?**

Your host smiles at you.
His long, sharp, teeth glint in the moonlight.
He walks towards you.

You back away, but...

...there's no escape!

You wake next morning. Was it all a nightmare?

You feel weak. Your neck is sore.
There are bite marks on your neck!

Your host is a vampire!

He will visit you again and again.

In the end, you will become a vampire, too – doomed to drink the blood of others forever.

13

THE UNDEAD

Someone bitten by a vampire becomes weak and pale. They will seem to die.

But then they will rise from their grave to drink blood!

Vampires are undead.

VAMPIRE SPOTTING

There are no real vampires. But there are plenty of vampire stories. In some places, people still believe in vampires.

People say a vampire sleeps in the day in its coffin.

A vampire must avoid sunlight – so it has very pale skin. A vampire has long, sharp, pointed teeth – to bite its victim!

Vampires must drink blood. They come out only at night to hunt for victims. Some can turn into animals, such as bats.

In some countries people think vampires are not pale.

They are red from the blood they drink!

STOP A VAMPIRE!

In some countries, people are afraid dead bodies will turn into vampires.

They believe there are ways to stop a corpse coming back as a vampire:

- Tie the arms together.

- Nail the body to the coffin.

- Drive a stake through the brain or heart.

If you fail, the vampire will rise from its grave at night!

Throw rice or seeds in the vampire's path. A vampire must count every single grain before it can pass.

You need to keep the vampire busy until sunrise. Sunlight turns vampires to dust.

VAMPIRE HUNTING

When the vampire returns to its grave, a vampire hunter can destroy it.

A crucifix will keep vampires away.
A vampire cannot go near a crucifix.

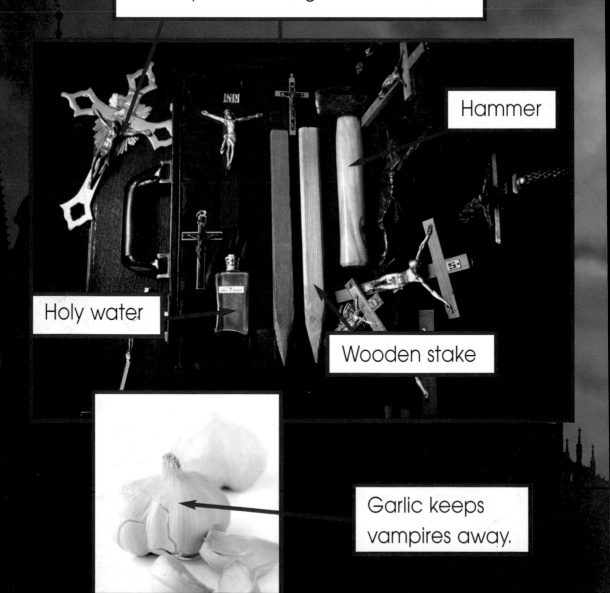

Hammer

Holy water

Wooden stake

Garlic keeps vampires away.

Holy water can destroy vampires. Holy water is normal water that has been blessed by a priest.

A vampire hunter can hammer a wooden stake through a vampire's heart to destroy it.

A vampire hunter can also burn a vampire's body to destroy it.

VAMPIRES ON FILM

Vampire stories are popular. There are many films and TV shows about vampires.

Buffy the Vampire Slayer is a TV show about a teenage vampire hunter. In the show, vampires can look like normal people.

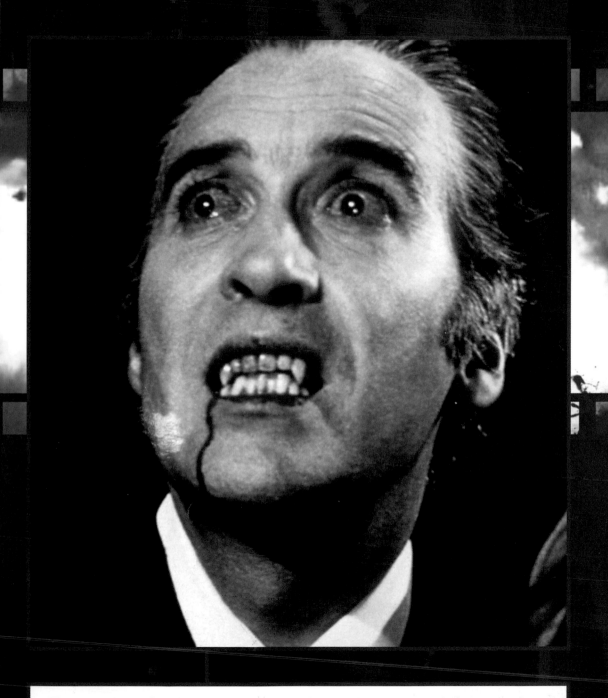

The actor, Christopher Lee played the most famous movie vampire of all – Count Dracula. He wore special contact lenses to make his eyes look blood red.

THE REAL DRACULA

Dracula's name comes from a real person called Vlad the Third of Romania. He was sometimes called Vlad Dracula.

Vlad lived in a castle in Romania.

Some stories say that he was a vampire.

Vlad was also called Vlad the Impaler. This was because he had criminals and his enemies impaled on spikes.

Once, Vlad impaled 30,000 people in one day. He put his table by the spikes and had dinner as he watched his victims die.

VAMPIRES: FACT OR FICTION?

**Why have people believed in vampires?
Dead bodies hold a clue.**

Dead people can turn dark red or purple.
It looks as if they have fed on blood.

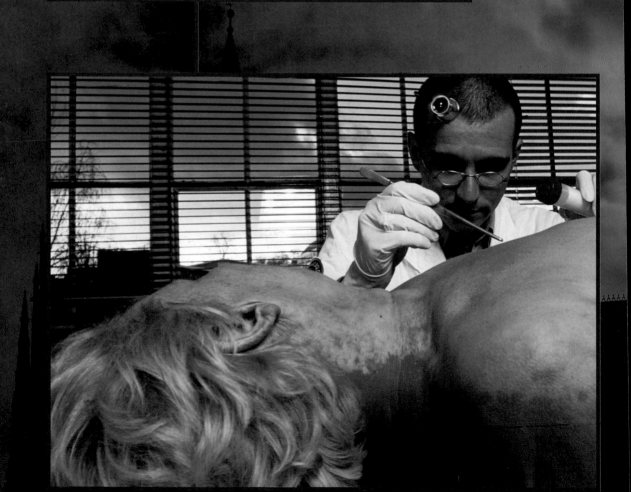

After death, the gums shrink.
This makes the teeth look longer.

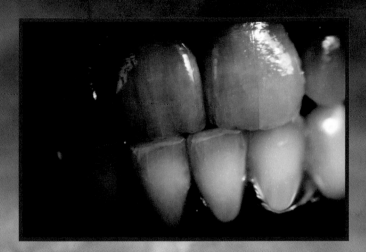

There is a rare disease that makes people easily hurt by sunlight. People with the disease stay out of the sun, so they are very pale.

The disease can also turn their fingernails and teeth blood-red.

REAL-LIFE BLOODSUCKERS

Even though human vampires don't exist, vampires are real! Some animals drink blood to live.

Vampire bats feed on blood.

They use their fangs to make tiny holes in animals.

Then they lick up the blood.

The vampire finch is a small bird. It lives on islands in the Pacific Ocean. During the dry season, it drinks the blood of sea birds!

The biggest danger from bloodsuckers is the mosquito. It is a tiny insect that can carry the deadly disease malaria. A mosquito doesn't have teeth like a vampire. It stabs a tiny tube into its prey and sucks the blood up.

Tube

Blood

NEED TO KNOW WORDS

blessed When a priest makes something holy.

coffin A box that holds a dead body.

contact lens A small circle of glass or plastic put into the eye to help a person see.

corpse A dead body.

crucifix A model of Jesus Christ on a cross.

dry season A time of year when not much rain falls.

fang A long, sharp tooth.

glint A small flash of light reflected from a shiny surface.

grave A hole in the ground where a dead body is buried.

host A person who lets guests stay in their home.

impale To push a sharp stake or spike through something.

malaria A disease caused by the bite of some mosquitoes.

prey An animal that is hunted by another animal as food.

priest Someone whose job is to lead religious services.

Romania A country in south-east Europe.

shrink To get smaller.

stake A wooden stick with a point at one end. It is thought to be the best way to kill a vampire.

undead A person who is dead but can still move around.

victim A person that something bad happens to.

VAMPIRES AROUND THE WORLD

- In China there are stories of a vampire called a kuangshi. It has bright red eyes, sharp fangs and is covered in green hair.

- In India, stories tell of a female vampire called a churel. It has a black tongue and back-to-front feet.

- Malaysia has stories of a vampire called a bajang. This is a demon that can be kept in a jar and used to hurt enemies.

VAMPIRES ONLINE

Websites

http://library.thinkquest.org/5482/
Some general information on vampire stories

http://science.howstuffworks.com/vampire.htm
The history of vampire stories around the world

http://kids.nationalgeographic.com/Animals/CreatureFeature/Vampire-bat
Facts about vampire bats

INDEX